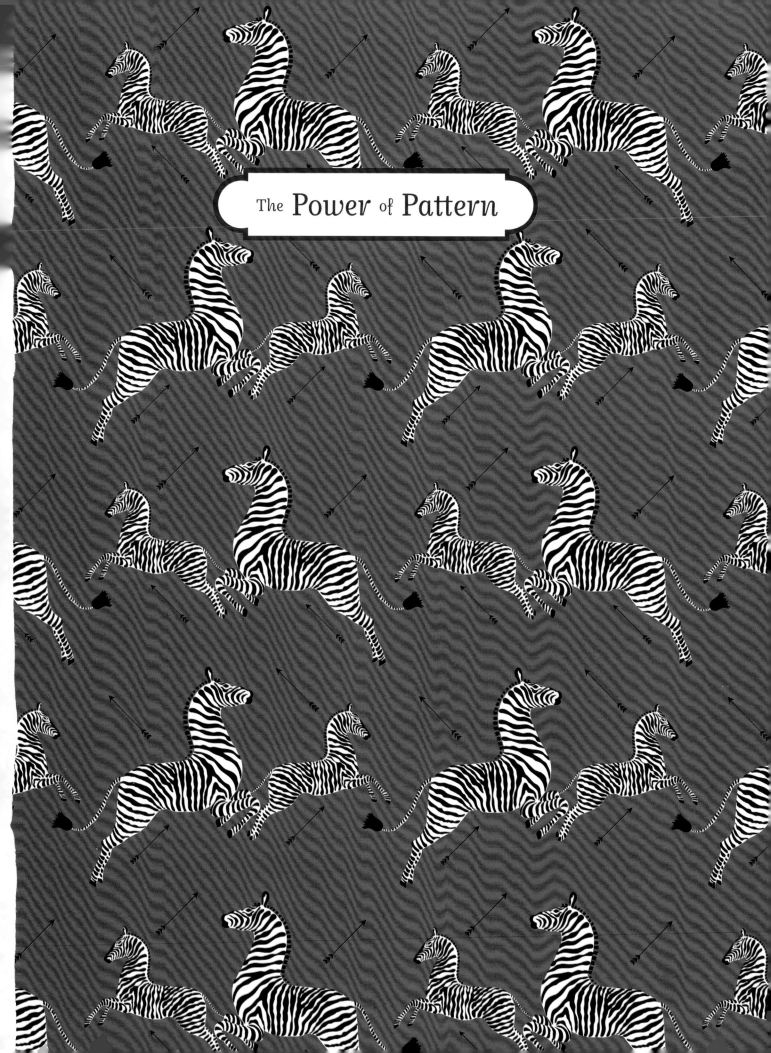

The Power of Pattern

The Power of Pattern

INTERIORS AND INSPIRATION: A RESOURCE GUIDE

Susanna Salk

RIZZOLI
NEW YORK

Paris London Milan

Contents

Susanna Salk

I never used to think much about the patterns in textiles and wallpapers. I appreciated them the way you do the scenery in a compelling play: you admire it but your focus remains on the cast of characters, which in a room consists of the furniture, art, lighting fixtures, and accessories. But over the years patterns started to dazzle me. After being exposed to so many memorable interiors—whether in person visiting a designer's home, or virtually, via my design feed on Pinterest or Instagram—it eventually became clear that the common element in a fabulous room, besides fearlessness and function, was, more often than not, pattern.

Pattern has been part of every designer's arsenal since the dawn of decorating. As most will tell you, a great room has layers and there's no better way to add a visual and literal layer than through a pattern. Be it on wallpaper, textiles, or floor covering, pattern brings a unique liveliness to a room. It was during the first episode of the BBC's *Sherlock* that I went from being an ardent admirer of patterns to being the author of a book on patterns. Normally I couldn't keep my eyes off Benedict Cumberbatch's brilliant Sherlock Holmes. But over the course of one scene in Sherlock's apartment at 221B Baker Street, he began to

be upstaged. I froze my screen to ponder Zoffany's moody and gorgeous fleur-de-lis wallpaper across one wall in his living room. I was smitten with how perfectly it captured the dark and quirky depths of Holmes's world and mind. I called my editor, Ellen Nidy at Rizzoli, who has shepherded me through nine other book titles and told her, "We need to do a book on pattern and show the unique ways designers play with them." She agreed, especially with my passion for celebrating the patterns themselves (as so often the designs are relegated to small rectangular swatches in magazines and books). "Let's make the patterns the stars of the show and run them as full pages," I ventured. We decided to divide the book into chapters according to key pattern categories. That way, if you needed inspiration and information on, say, stripes, you could flip to that chapter. Or toile. Floral. Animals, and so on until we had twelve of them. There's even an Iconic chapter featuring many of the greatest and most cherished patterns. I'm sure I've forgotten a few and neglected many more. I will confess that every pattern and room shown here is one I love and would happily live with: that was my criteria as I delved into a year of pattern sleuthing. I hope you'll be inspired by the ones I have chosen. They deserve, in my mind, to be center stage.

Background: Navarre Wallpaper from Zoffany

Inset: Great Toile in Lipstick Pink on Oyster from Bennison Fabrics

Floral

To think of florals as merely lighthearted is to vastly underestimate their power. They have surprising variety—from demure to dramatic—which can bring many moods to a room. With roots stemming from twelfth-century Asia, floral prints eventually traveled to the West, along the way exposing the rest of the world to flower patterns of every variety. Before long, florals' design tendrils had grown and blossomed into a worldwide presence that celebrated traditional bouquets, such as clutches of nosegay, as well as modern pops of single blossoms. In patterns, their verdant shapes can be highlighted by backgrounds as varied as the vases they're conventionally displayed in, from basic white to a more unexpected deep brown or even black.

"I love working with floral patterns because they are a perfect starting point for a richly layered and nuanced room," says New York interior designer Colleen Bashaw. "I think of them as a feminine point of view into which I can layer the right amount of masculine to create a fine balance."

Sometimes the stem or vine is more predominant in the pattern than the actual flower; sometimes the repeat is as crowded as a spring meadow; in others, it's as orderly as a hedge. Regardless, it's almost impossible not to feel better when surrounded by florals. "Floral patterns in design date back to the earliest cultures because they provide strong and emotive life-affirming images of beauty," says Los Angeles-based interior and textile designer Timothy Corrigan.

Florals' rich symbolism has mood-altering effects as well. New York interior designer Frank de Biasi says, "Flowers themselves instantly brighten a room, adding warmth and natural beauty. Some spaces can handle elaborate floral patterns, such as a large sofa or garden room, while intimate spaces like a powder room do better with touches throughout." Even just a hint of flora soothes and inspires.

Self-proclaimed gardener at heart, Los Angeles interior and textile designer Suzanne Rheinstein says: "I love using block-printed linens on the wrong side—so you just barely see the outlines of the flowers that look like they were painted with watercolors."

Background: Charlotte in Rose Indien by Manuel Canovas from Cowtan & Tout

Inset: Indian Arbre in Hyacinth by Schumacher

In the dining room turned game central of her
New Orleans home, Sara Ruffin Costello juxtaposes
the unexpected with the classic by pairing a
Ping-Pong table with a sofa covered in Lee Jofa's
classic chintz Mayfield Cotton in Cream.

Peonies in Pink
from Brett Design

Designer Colleen Bashaw loves Peonies in Pink for its
content and scale: "It creates a wonderful surprise
in a small powder room. I love how girlie and happy
it is—perfect for a summer house."

Schumacher's iconic Pyne Hollyhock in Charcoal gets a modern vibe when paired with Kelly Wearstler's Crescent wallpaper pattern in Ebony Cream in Jane Scott Hodges's New Orleans study. "After I installed the draperies in Hollyhock, I waited for the delayed order of a more subdued wallpaper," recalls Hodges. "Then I came across the fabulous Crescent paper and decided it could be a perfect combination and took a leap of faith! Somehow the riotous mix creates a perfect environment for a cozy sitting room."

Three distinct patterns give an exotic cohesiveness to
a bathroom wall. All three are by Schumacher: Taj Trellis
in Jaipur Blue on the ceiling, Topkapi in Peacock on the
upper wall, and Samovar in Peacock on the lower wall.

<small>Opposite:</small> Topkapi in Peacock
by Martyn Lawrence Bullard for Schumacher

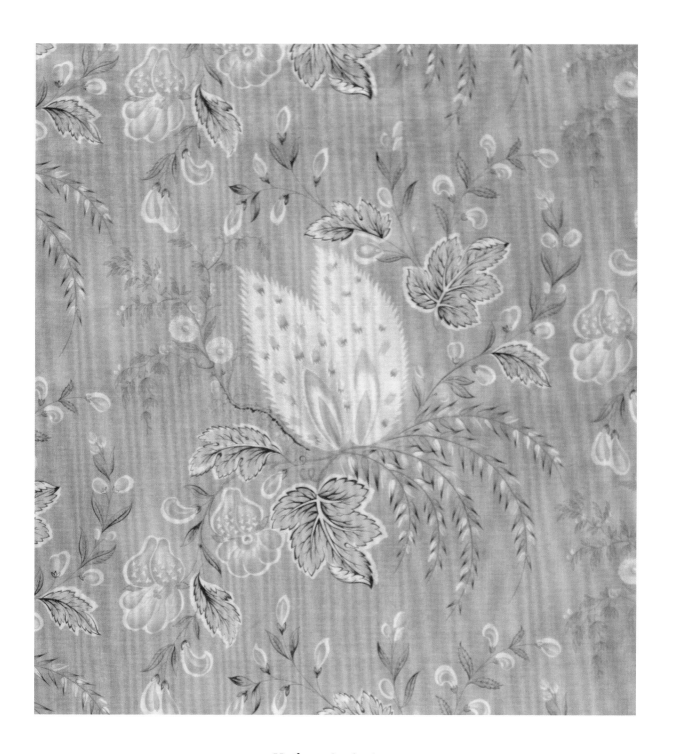

Hatley print in Aqua
from Suzanne Tucker Home

"With its stylized leaves, trailing vines, and flowering
branches, my Hatley print in Aqua provided the perfect
springboard to create a young girl's bedroom," says
designer Suzanne Tucker of Tucker & Marks Design.
The pattern is charming and fanciful with multiple layers,
giving it a fresh yet sophisticated look."

Indian Arbre in Spring
from Schumacher Classics Collection

The big bloom scale of Indian Arbre in Hyacinth
by Schumacher beautifully blurs the boundaries
of this bathroom and makes the formal lines of
its accessories feel more playful.

Penelope in Gris, Turquoise by Manuel Canovas
from Cowtan & Tout

Roses in Shocking Pink on Oyster
from Bennison Fabrics

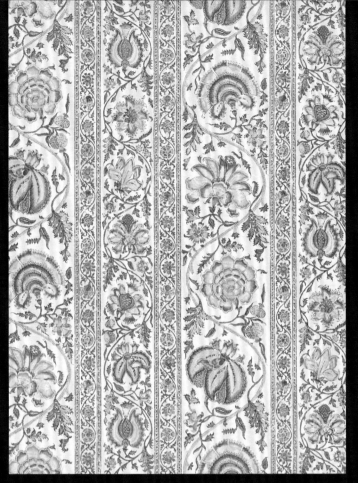

Coromandel Grey Rust on Beige from Bennison Fabrics

Heritage Floral in Multi by Lilly Pulitzer for Lee Jofa

Elizabeth in Multi Rouge by Alessandra Branca for Schumacher

Huntington Gardens in Bleu Marine
by Timothy Corrigan for Schumacher

St. Antoine in Off Black on Bone by Farrow & Ball

Casimir Velvet in Black by Colefax and Fowler from Cowtan & Tout

Bermuda Blossoms in Jet
by Mary McDonald for Schumacher

27

Animal

Whether mimicking a real animal's fur or shell (think zebra, leopard, or tortoise) or depicting animals in fanciful poses and colorations (be they elephants, birds, monkeys, fish, rabbits, horses, or even turtles), animal-themed textile patterns bring a playful sophistication no matter how or where they frolic in the house. Animal patterns don't need to be relegated to a child's room! With their regal shapes, they can populate a glamorous living room as well as a cozy kitchen. Their unexpected appearance when they're brought inside always delights.

"There is a chaos and an order in nature that strikes a balance I find more interesting than other simpler geometric patterns," says interior and textile designer Celerie Kemble. "Animal patterns resonate with a beauty that is usable and classic despite having an intrinsic, almost iconic glamour. I love using them in my design because they supply a bold movement that the eye doesn't tire of and a beautiful graphic element that is not too literal."

Whether striving for realism or fantasy, animal patterns have long struck designers' fancies. "When I was a teenager in Paris, I had a friend whose grandfather's house had been done by Elsie de Wolfe," recalls New York-based designer Robert Couturier. "There was a spiral staircase linking one of the upper floors to the children's apartments that had a carpet in a zebra pattern. That pattern going up gave such life, movement, and originality that it stayed in my mind and when I became a designer I began to use animals in patterns frequently. I think the animal element is always within us, emotional, strong, and quite subconscious. Whether it's a red and white toile of cows in a field, Braquenie's La Ménagerie of zoological gardens, or Schumacher's Singeries with playful monkeys, everything with animals feels truly happy!"

Background: Napoleon Bee Wallpaper in Black and Gold on Red from Timorous Beasties

Inset: Paired with the wooden dresser, Caledonia in Grasshopper from Schuyler Samperton Textiles, with its cheerful birds and verdant colorway, gives the feeling of being inside an enchanted forest.

In Anne Maxwell Foster's country home, the design duo Tilton Fenwick (of which Foster is cofounder) chose Pierre Frey's Ismaelia for the banquettes and Scalamandre's Tigre Velvet for the pillows. "We are big believers in pattern on pattern and when those patterns also happen to be animal prints, then the fabrics really sing," says Foster. "Ismaelia is both traditional and whimsical and Tigre is the most timeless animal print fabric and works with any pattern and in any room."

The Leopard AX carpet in Stock colorway from Stark gives
Amanda Lindroth's bedroom just enough fiery foundation. "Where does
one start with regard to my not-so-secret love for animal prints?"
says Lindroth. "I hope my attraction veers more closely to Madeleine Castaing
than Jackie Collins, but all the same bring them on!"

Opposite: When designer Peter Dunham needed to give this viewless office some
height and drama, he created Gattopardo (here in the Siberiano colorway),
inspired by a mohair car blanket from the 1920s that he bought years before.
"Animal prints always have a provocative sexiness for me," says Dunham.

Singeries in Multi on White
from Schumacher

Animals on patterns can be fanciful rather than literal.
Schumacher's Singeries pattern becomes an
intriguing focal point, beckoning visitors to come ever
closer to see what the monkey business is all about.
Interior design by Mallory Mathison Glenn.

Versailles Grand in Pink and Chartreuse Multi
from the Folie Collection, Cole and Son

"Versailles Grand from Cole and Son with its perfectly balanced
compositions is a favorite wallpaper of mine," says designer Bennett
Leifer. "I love the crisp white ground and colorful imagery. It feels
current and exciting, but is based in tradition. I wanted the feeling of this
space to evolve past the clean white stone and to transition into colorful
accents in a logical way and this pattern made that transition."

Calypso in Marine by Manuel Canovas
from Cowtan & Tout

When it came to her own home, designer Katie Ridder had a myriad of choices but her Turtle Bay in Prussian Blue seemed perfect for the guest bathroom. "I love animals in patterns because they are part of nature. They bring whimsy, character, movement, and liveliness to a pattern— they literally animate my wallpapers and fabrics."

Balabina Mariinsky in Velvet Red from Cole and Son

Tortoise in Natural by Celerie Kemble for Schumacher

El Morocco in Espresso from Scalamandre

Le Jardin de Mysore in Exotique
from Pierre Frey

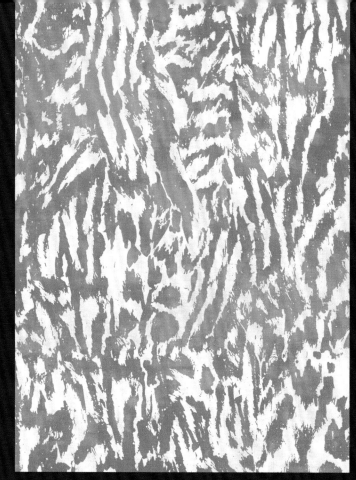

Feline in Stone by Celerie Kemble for Schumacher

Jembala Wool Crewel from Clarence House

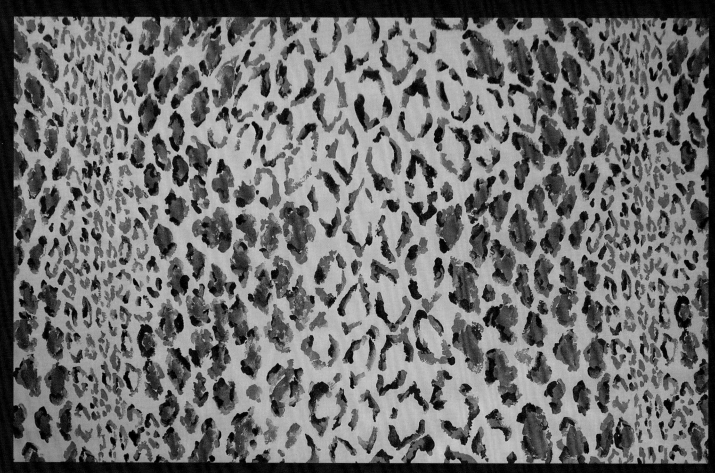

Sabu in Red/Rose by Rose Cumming

Reverse Phoenix in Mid Blue on Oyster
from Bennison Fabrics

Chinoiserie

During the seventeenth and eighteenth centuries, Europeans became fascinated with Asian cultures and traditions: China was a mysterious, faraway place few had ever seen. But as traders and tourists eventually traveled eastward and stories and sketchbooks of Oriental designs made their way back to Europe, "Chinoiserie"—a French word meaning "in the Chinese style"—joined the vernacular, as well as the homes, of the wealthy. Scenes of the Orient on textiles and wallpapers, distinguished by classic climbing branches, lush landscapes, fanciful pavilions, and fabulous birds, evoked exotic luxury and divine destinations.

Today, there is nothing dated about worldly chinoiserie. Mixing it in your rooms alongside more modern pieces has the poppy panache of pairing your grandmother's chic pearls with your favorite blue jeans.

"There is nothing I love more than the playful whimsy of chinoiserie in all of its forms to lighten up a room," says interior and textile designer Mary McDonald, who is based in Los Angeles. "It creates an interesting tension to juxtapose the delight of chinoiserie with modernity in other patterns and forms."

While chinoiserie wallpaper patterns can be as costly as a couture outfit (installations often involve hand-painted, original designs on custom colorways and backgrounds of your choosing), the spirit of chinoiserie can also be captured through more affordable prints. The effect will always be transportive.

"The lure of the exotic has always captivated me," says Los Angeles designer Hutton Wilkinson. "Tony Duquette taught me that the subtle juxtaposition of Oriental and Occidental is an essential for creating true beauty. Chinoiserie continually leaves me spellbound and longing for my favorite part of the world, the East."

Background: Yangtze River in Onyx from Schumacher

Inset: The grays of the hand-painted design from de Gournay, Jardinières & Citrus Trees wallpaper (in a custom colorway on gray metallic xuan paper), offer a soft, feminine formality.

Based on an original Elsie de Wolfe design for the Condé Nast ballroom, this Ming Garden wallpaper by Gracie was customized by designer Alex Papachristidis by blowing up its scale (and adding a few purple peonies and butterflies along the way) for a decidedly modern and glamorous effect. Interior design by Alex Papachristidis.

48

Serene whites and shades of gray look extra
chic layered with the wallpaper pattern Hampton Garden
by Gracie. Interior design by Mary McDonald.

Opposite: The tangerine drapery of Chinois Palace by
Mary McDonald for Schumacher uplifts and accentuates
the orange walls, lending the furniture in the room
both warmth and timelessness.

Pagoda in Saffron
from Katie Ridder

Above: Katie Ridder's Pagoda in Persimmon offers another
rich layer to this sitting area without competing with
the lively art and colorful banquette. It's a perfect example
of how a beautiful pattern doesn't distract but enhances.
Interior design by Katie Ridder.

Pattern can be counted on to be as lively and colorful an accessory
as fresh flowers or a collection of china. Here the delicious
Imperial Dragon in Coral and Turquoise from Thibaut proves why.

Opposite: The hand-painted Earlham pattern on emerald
green-dyed silk from de Gournay is used in this dining room
by designer Melissa Warner Rothblum. "I love how
chinoiserie is classic and traditional yet can feel modern
and fresh when paired with unexpected colors."

Even a colorful chinoiserie still feels delicate, allowing you to pull in a mix of surrounding hues, from curtains to chairs, violet to gold. Here, Jardinières & Citrus Trees on Natural Mica 73 Metallic Xuan Paper from de Gournay as interpreted by designer Ashley Whittaker.

A chinoiserie pattern can animate a room full of strong
solids without losing the focus. Here the punctuations
of blue in the Ming Village wallpaper by Gracie are beautifully
echoed in the velvet chairs. Interior design by White Webb.

Opposite: Ming Village, hand-painted Chinese scenic wallpaper
from Gracie

Pearl River in Blush
from Schumacher

Paradiso in Sungold
from Fromental

Paradiso in Fern with embroidery
from Fromental

Hand-painted Askew design on Apple Green
Williamsburg from de Gournay

Les Fetes D'Orient in Brown from Clarence House

Palownia in Blue Oxyde from Zuber & Cie

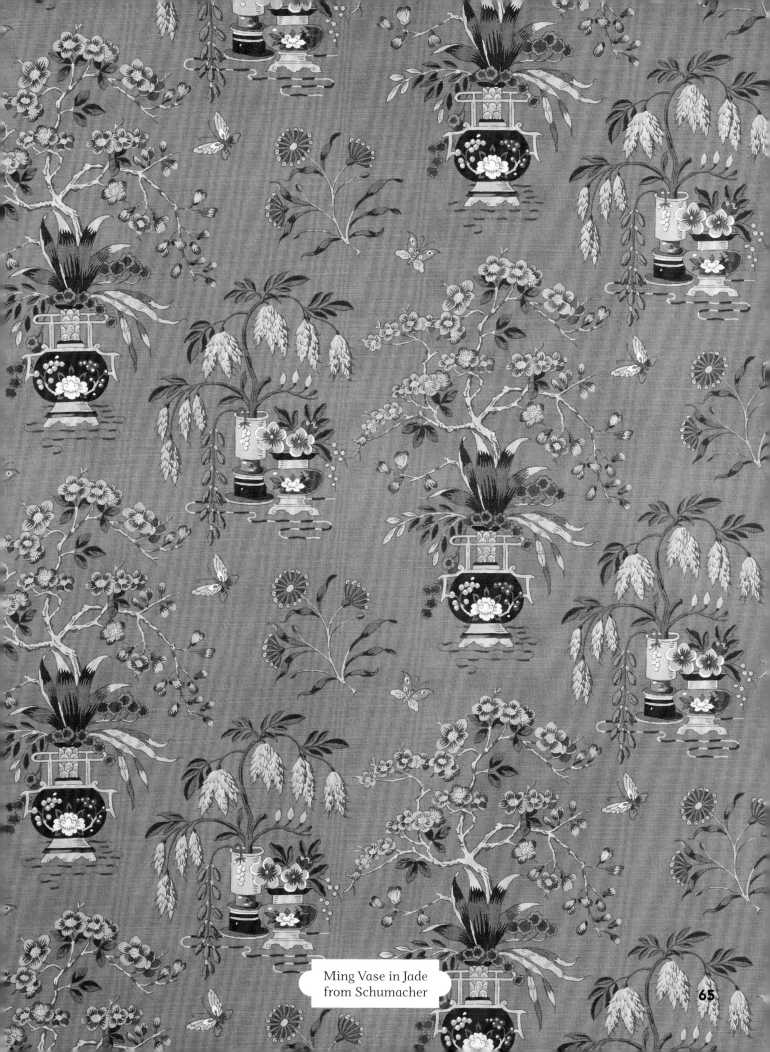

Ming Vase in Jade
from Schumacher

Hand-painted Jardinières & Citrus Trees on
Custom Gray Metallic Silk from de Gournay

Chi'en Dragon Linen Print in Persimmon
from Scalamandre

Gondola in Teal and Amber
from the Frontier Collection of Cole and Son

Nanjing in Porcelain from Schumacher

Nanjing in Mandarin from Scalamandre

Nature

CHAPTER
4

"When it comes to color and pattern, nature is never wrong," says New York-based interior and textile designer Philip Gorrivan. "Patterns help create narrative and authenticity in any space, especially patterns inspired by nature. I like to introduce pattern through wall coverings, whether it's walls or ceilings, and then add a layer of fabric—curtains, upholstery, and rugs. Nothing should ever match, but it should relate."

With organic elements such as butterflies, birds and branches, or fishes and ferns, patterns with natural elements can create rooms that soothe and feel like sanctuaries. "I've always been drawn to patterns from nature—from the classically rendered acanthus leaves on ancient Corinthian columns to the delicate web of jasmine vines in a William Morris weaving," says Los Angeles-based interior and textile designer Schuyler Samperton. "To me, patterns inspired by nature have a kind of wild romanticism that's rooted in both history and our most primitive selves. Using them is like creating your own beautiful, private forest." With patterns that isolate individual elements of nature's bounty, such as clouds, waves, shells, or trees, the ordinary can look extraordinary, and in turn elevate your inside world to something even more beautiful than what lies outside its walls.

Background: Waikiki Green on Oyster from Bennison Fabrics

Inset: Children's bedtime dreams can become enchanted when they are surrounded by nature's enchanting elements. Interior design by Maria Drattell.

70

In a sitting room, a hand-painted silk Prunus pattern from Fromental gives a Louis XVI chaise longue a verdant and playful touch. Interior design by Roman and Williams.

Designer Miles Redd proves that pattern, especially when
nature inspired, can elegantly envelope a bed like a canopy.
On walls, hand-painted Jardinières & Citrus Trees on
Natural Mica Metallic Silk wallpaper by de Gournay.

Opposite: Pattern is sometimes just the spice that's needed
to keep symmetry and tradition on its toes, as delightfully
proved in this bedroom via Cole and Son's Hummingbirds
pattern in Duck Egg. Interior design by Nathan Turner.

Designer Philip Gorrivan uses Josef Frank's Windows pattern (inspired by Frank's love of common houseplants) on a sofa as a way of bringing levity and light to a solid wall filled with weighty art.

Stairs are an ideal place to border with pattern as a counterpoint to the rail's architecture. Here Fern Tree from Schumacher seems like nature's version of the wood balusters. Interior design by Kate Maloney.

Opposite: Nothing makes a small room look bigger—or dreamier— than using a big pattern. "Nature-themed wallpaper immediately transports one into the magical, beautiful world of the elements," says the room's designer Fawn Galli.

This set of flora-and-fauna-filled panels was commissioned by designer Summer Thornton and painted by Allison Cosmos. "I love nature-inspired prints because who does print better than Mother Nature?" says Thornton. "I am always one for pattern on pattern so I like the way the busyness of the blue-and-white ginger jars plays off the looser pattern of the bamboo and birds. The subtle pattern of the wood floor adds to the effect and draws the eye through the arches. Everything about this tableau invites you into the home and gives a glimpse of what is to come."

Opposite: Designer Rita Konig didn't just choose this Perroquet pattern for her small entry because it was designed by her mother, Nina Campbell (and distributed by Osborne & Little). "It was a non-space before. The parrots were so whimsical, they gave it some fun and made it feel special. It was a winning combination, really."

Nuvolette by Fornasetti brings in a moody layer of drama while still acting like a neutral, ideal for a boy's room when navy seems too expected. "Fornasetti's clouds feel both graphic and powerful, as well as restful," says the room's designer, Philip Gorrivan. "There's nothing like sleeping in on a cloudy day!"

Wheat Flower in Strong Green Blue and Brown on Beige
from Bennison Fabrics

In architect Gil Schafer's master bedroom, Bennison
Fabrics's Wheat Flower in Strong Green Blue and Brown
on Beige was at first going to be used as an accent
pillow until friend and designer Miles Redd convinced
him to fearlessly use it on the walls. "The impact is
both strong and soothing," says Schafer.

On Jane Scott Hodges's den wall, Palm in Soft Grey on White from Cole and Son is the perfect playmate with Schumacher's bold Chiang Mai Dragon fabric on the sectional (and chair and throw pillow). The large-scaled leaves help integrate the bold artwork with the fearless yet inviting seating below.

A pattern detail can expertly highlight detail in furniture and thereby create additional visual excitement. Here, Carnival in Copper by Michael Szell for Christopher Farr Cloth as used by designer Colleen Bashaw.

Opposite: There's no more alluring allusion than making nature look like it's growing along your walls. Here, the magician is courtesy of Schumacher's Sinhala Sidewall in Jewel.

Aristote in Corail by Manuel Canovas
from Cowtan & Tout

Fishes in Blue Pearl on Tarnished Silver Paper with pearlescent antiquing
from de Gournay

Waves
from Gracie

Heliconia Dreamin' in Tropical, Leo de Janeiro Collection
from Jim Thompson Fabrics

Birdbranch Stripe Velvet in Black on Sea Blue
from Timorous Beasties

Fox Hollow in Document Natural from Schumacher

Bloomsbury Garden in Teal from Timorous Beasties

Mauritius in Ciel
from Pierre Frey

97

Cacao Vine in Mustard by Barry Dixon for Vervain

Zebra Palm Sisal in Black on Ivory from Schumacher

Lotus Garden in Jade from Schumacher

Fontainebleau from the Folie Collection
from Cole and Son

99

Coquina in Capri
from Scalamandre

Toile

In French, toile de Jouy literally means "cloth from Jouy-en-Josas," a town in the southwest suburbs of Paris where the fabric was first manufactured. Toile, originating in the late eighteenth century, conjures up an environment of relaxed elegance, privilege, and a touch of twee with its traditional pastoral scenes printed on cotton.

Toile's patterns have always offered the eye a chance to "armchair travel" across their romantic landscapes filled with everything from roses to ruins, ships to soldiers, dogs to donkeys, parrots to playful lovers.

Toile can be used conservatively to line the backs of chairs or the fronts of lampshades or the pattern can be used unexpectedly, such as on an accent wall behind a bed, bringing punctuation no matter how small the room's size.

Toile can also go bold: it is one of the few patterns that grows stronger in its repetition rather than redundant. One pattern can cover an entire room—from walls, to curtains to bedcovers—and make its inhabitant feel refreshed rather than weary. Perhaps it's the sense of space between its scenes that allows the eye to rest, or the relaxed nature of its subjects that induces a parallel mood in its beholder.

But toile is anything but somnolent. Many of its patterns are offered in color combinations that stylishly break out of the basic black, navy, or red on white traditional backgrounds: fuchsia on orange, turquoise on pistachio, rose on brown are just a few of the decidedly modern mixes to be found.

And it's not just using vivacious colors that can give toile a cheeky twist: designer Barry Dixon created an "Elway Hall" toile of men on horseback in top hats and tails that at first appears traditional in nature . . . until you notice that one gentleman is on a cell phone. No matter the pattern's dynamic, toile provides instant dynamism. "Toile patterns create interest in a room," says New York-based interior designer Alex Papachristidis. "Scenic patterns used with lighter color backgrounds tend to give great depth and dimension to a space. I love layered interiors. No matter the room's size, adding bold imagery with toile patterns instantly gives atmosphere."

Background: Balleroy in Rose by Manuel Canovas from Cowtan & Tout

Inset: Putting pattern on the wall behind the bed is a fanciful way to accentuate not only where you sleep but the linens you sleep in. Designer David Kleinberg puts Quadrille's Paradise Garden in Turquoise on Pistachio to beautiful effect on both.

Manuel Canovas's Bengale in Paprika is a bold colorway that never seems to lose its delight or usefulness. "This little girl's bedroom is a dormer with quite a few angles and slopes in the ceiling," says designer Angie Hranowsky. "In order to detract from that I chose a toile in her favorite color and covered the walls and ceiling. Now she can't help but be enveloped in this cozy and charming space."

Marine Toile in Indigo
from Schumacher

"I have always been a fan of the impact a toile pattern can
create in a small space," says designer Robert Passal.
"Juxtaposition was the key factor throughout this Miami home.
While the home itself is quite contemporary I worked with materials
that reflect the past to create visual interest and warmth.
The toile is printed on grass cloth, which in itself creates contrast."

Independence Toile in Red and Flag Blue on Tint
from Quadrille

Befitting a summer house in Maine, Independence Toile
from Quadrille depicting George Washington at the
reins of a leopard-drawn chariot (taken from a 1783
British printed fabric) is used with seamless abandon in
one colorway on the walls and another on the daybed.
Interior design by John Fondas and John Knott.

Jardin du Luxembourg in Abricot by Manuel Canovas
from Cowtan & Tout

La Musardiere in Manganese by Manuel Canovas
from Cowtan & Tout

Skylake Toile in Black and White by Serena & Lily

La Menagerie from the Braquenie Collection by Pierre Frey

Elway Toile in Mahogany on Celadon
from Barry Dixon for Vervain

Shengyou Toile in Iris
from Schumacher

Paisley

The paisley symbol was called *buta* or *botah* in Persian, meaning "flower." It can also be traced to Celtic tradition and its Western name comes from the patterned shawls that were manufactured in the town of Paisley, Scotland, in the 1800s.

Paisley's semblances are many: its swirling shape can read as a curved droplet, a feather, or fig. It also exudes a multitude of connotations: mystery, due to its exotic origins; psychedelic funk because of its fervent faddish following in the late 1960s, and privilege, thanks to the well-heeled European fashion houses like Etro who still trot out paisley on the runway as a dandy mascot.

"In my interior design work I have always used the language and layering of pattern to create an exotic atmosphere with warmth and comfort," says New York-based interior designer Charlotte Moss. "A Scottish paisley, a French toile, a kilim rug, or a hand-blocked Indian tablecloth are suggestive of a well-traveled life and one willing to experiment with combinations.

Decorating has the ability to transport—and the layering of pattern achieves that. Like a woman well dressed from head to toe, so should a room be great from ceiling to floor."

Paisley's presence in the home also multi-tasks: it's a pattern that can work both as a neutral and as a vivacious accent—it all depends upon the complexity of its coloration. In fact, for such a steadfast symbol, its variations are surprisingly endless: whether in a singular or a more crowded repeat, via softer hues with sensible shapes or bold, oversize ones, paisley's power should not be underestimated.

"I really love paisleys because they are the most exotic of designs," says textile and interior designer Peter Dunham. "They are part of what I call ethnic geometrics. Their layout is pleasingly regular but the shapes are fundamentally sensual. It's a very easy shape and grid to live with."

Whether stretched luxuriously along a wall or accenting a pillow, paisley always feels right at home.

Background: Jaipur Paisley in Persimmon from Scalamandre

Inset: As exotic as paisleys are, they can also easily work as a neutral given their even tone. Here, a chair is covered in Isfahan in Charcoal and the cushion in Isfahan Stripe in Raspberry, both by Peter Dunham Textiles.

As long as the palette is compatible with its surroundings, a colorful paisley can act as a perfect backdrop for even more exotic layering. Interior design by Fabrizio Rollo.

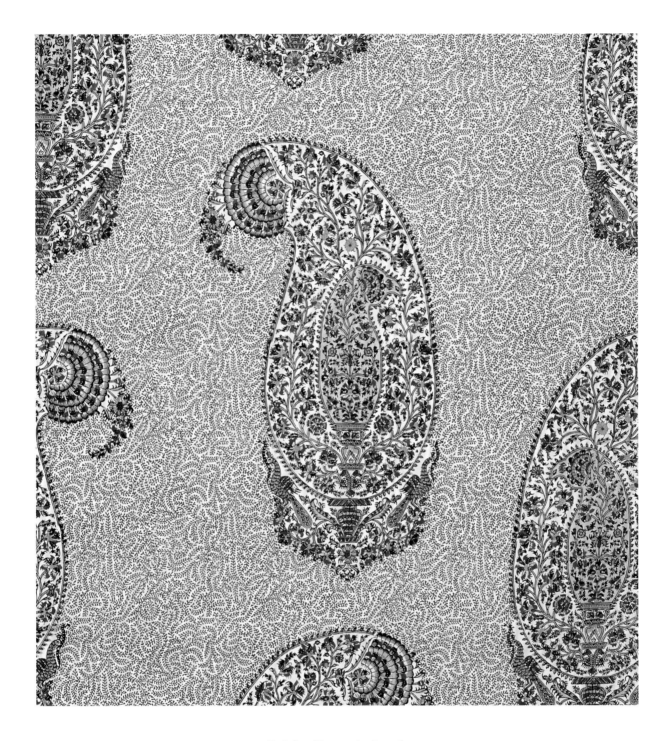

Paisley Parrot in Jewel
from Soane Britain

A bedroom becomes a delicious haven of pinks and
paisleys and parrots via Soane Britain's Paisley Parrot
in Jewel. Interior design by Lulu Lytle.

Shirala Paisley in Aqua from Schumacher

Kashmir Paisley in Tea Green
from Peter Dunham Textiles

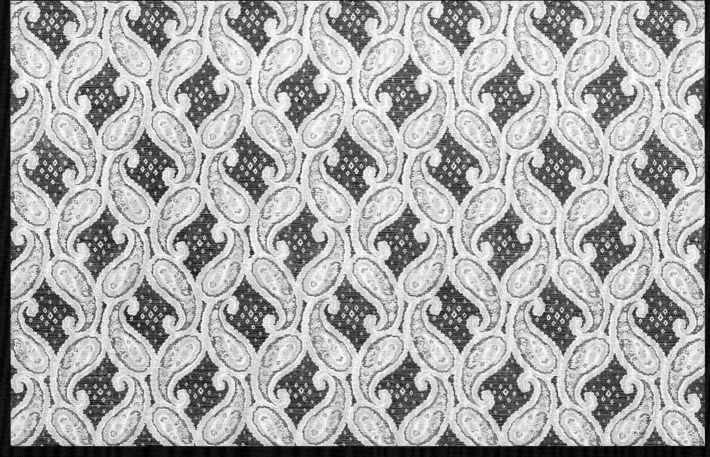

Calicut Paisley in Indigo on Beige from Bennison Fabrics

"I love the romance of paisley," says Martyn Lawrence Bullard, who designed this room using his Pasha Paisley in Taupe pattern for Schumacher. "The undulating designs have a magical quality and the symmetry of the pattern appeals to my design sense. Paisley adds drama, power, and endless inspiration to so many decorative periods."

124

Rajasthan Paisley in Jewel
from Schumacher

125

Cambay Paisley in Parrot
from Schumacher

Blakewater in Red from Jane Churchill
for Cowtan & Tout

Katara Paisley in Delft from Schumacher

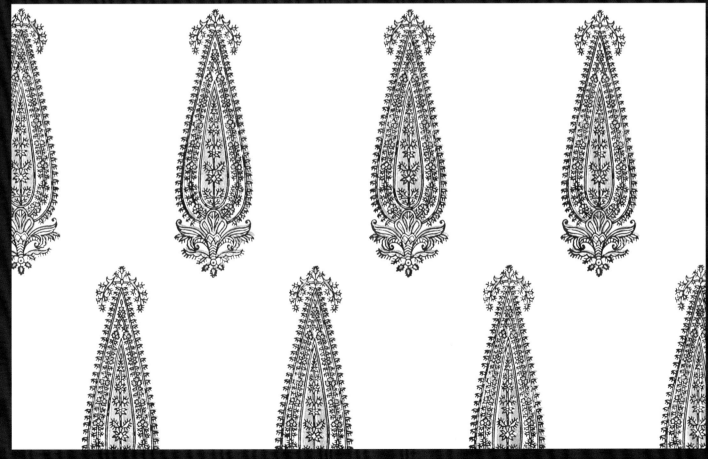

Ratana Peacock from John Robshaw

Damask

Long possessing status as a luxury fabric, damask got its name when Western traders were first able to purchase it in Damascus, a popular textile-trading hub along the Silk Road during the Middle Ages. What makes damask distinct is that its pattern is woven into the cloth, so the fabric is always reversible (fabrics that use multiple colors and are not reversible are called brocades).

"I love damasks," says Italian designer Alessandra Branca. "I love playing them against more current modern items and using them in unexpected ways: either on a modern chair or by upholstering the walls with them or juxtaposing them with contemporary art or photography. I always wash them to soften the material and make them feel warmer and less high style." Typically woven of silk, damask has a pattern that beautifully reflects light and shows an elegant variation in tone. While we tend to associate damask with very traditional, if not somber interiors, textile companies such as London-based Timorous Beasties as well as Branca's own collection for Schumacher, are determined to maintain damask's relevancy with punchier, more modern patterns and colors.

Background: Luciana Damask in Raspberry from Scalamandre

Inset: A damask can unify large-scale pieces in a room with dignity and grace. Here designer Markham Roberts uses Bennison Fabrics's Lorenzo in Brown on Oyster, its splendid shapes echoing the curves of the chandelier.

Designer Alessandra Branca infused
a traditional damask pattern
with a chic shot of color, then coated
a bedroom in it while adding touches
of chinoiserie. The result is pure
glamour and unexpected modernity.
The pattern is Anna Damask in
Acid Green by Alessandra Branca
for Schumacher.

"We thought this bold blue damask-patterned wallpaper would be the perfect thing for a tiny bedroom that could benefit from a little drama," says designer Gil Schafer. "We knew that the visual punch of Raphaello paper (in Delft from Cowtan & Tout) would more than make up for what the room lacked in size and scale. Plus, it made the space incredibly cozy in the end."

A simple entry hall is transformed into a destination worthy of any arrival, thanks to the boldly elegant and graphic Khitan wallpaper in Black and Ivory by Nina Campbell distributed by Osborne & Little.

Khitan in Black and Ivory by Nina Campbell distributed by Osborne & Little

Melograno Prussian Blue/Rouge by Alessandra Branca for Schumacher

Petrouchka, Mariinsky Collection
from Cole and Son

Ikat

"Before I was a textile designer, I was a painter," says New York textile and carpet designer Madeline Weinrib. "Ikat feels so similar to painting. The jagged edges remind me of brushstrokes on a canvas, and the dye imperfections recall the drips and splatter of paint, which gives the fabric a kind of soul or poetry. Like a beautiful painting, ikat looks wonderful anywhere."

Created with silk or cotton fabric, ikat is probably one of the oldest forms of textile decoration. It involves a weaving style that is common to many world cultures, but is most prevalent in Indonesia where it originated. What makes it unique is that the threads are dyed before they are woven into textiles and this ultimately produces the characteristic "blurriness" of the pattern, reflecting the difficulty the weaver has in lining up the dyed yarns.

It's this very challenge that gives ikat its cherished characteristic and its undefined quality, which makes it more appealing to many. "Ikats often have bold geometric shapes that are softer than contemporary geometric patterns and therefore more versatile," says Lisa Fine of Lisa Fine Textiles. "I usually choose ones with rich vibrant jewel tones."

When used in interiors ikats feel both dressed up and chicly casual. Their rustic weave can make a modern room feel cozier without compromising its elegance or can give a more traditional room an exotic uptick. Ikats look stunning as the focal point—stretched across a console, or, as curtains as well as in a supporting role: punctuating a lampshade or pillow. "I love the art of the ikat," says Los Angeles interior and textile designer Martyn Lawrence Bullard. "The wonderful, exotic nature of these tribal fabrics is always striking and often individual, depending on who makes them. I find they work in many interiors, from the most formal to the most relaxed, always adding a certain element of exotic style and luxury."

Background: Samarkand Ikat II in Porcelain from Schumacher

Inset: Designer Lilly Bunn transforms a bergère chair from fussy to family friendly with Madeline Weinrib's Mu Ikat in Purple with her Stripe in Purple on the cushion. But Gracie's Hampton Garden pattern on the walls ensures that the dining space feels dressed for guests.

Designer Michelle Nussbaumer proves how ikat
should never be relegated to only a pillow or two.
By continuing her Royal Palais Jamais Ikat throughout
her son's bedroom in Gstaad, a chic coziness is created.

Ikat jibes so well with other patterns and often helps connect the more fanciful ones (such as Fromental's Willow on the walls) with the more serious ones (see the floor covering) in a small space. Interior design by Katie Ridder.

Opposite: In a large space ikat can hold its own, and alongside other patterns in its same colorway it can almost be used as a neutral. Interior design by Kirsten Kelli.

Darya Ikat in Sky
by Martyn Lawrence Bullard for Schumacher

Martyn Lawrence Bullard uses his Darya Ikat for
Schumacher both on the walls and the backs of chairs
in this sitting area for an effect that feels both antiquated
and modern, thanks to its contemporary and geometric
pattern. It's the juxtaposition that makes the room zing.
Old-world portraits never looked so fresh!

Adras Silk Ikat
from Bermingham & Company

Ikat can feel fabulously feminine as articulated by
Adras Silk from Bermingham & Company on the dining
room chairs. Interior design by Amanda Nisbet.

Daphne in Celery
from Madeline Weinrib

Purple Luce Ikat from Madeline Weinrib   Bali Isle French Blue on Tint from Quadrille

Dashwood from Madeline Weinrib

Kashgar Ikat in Carbon and Teak from Schumacher

Vino Brown and Iris from Madeline Weinrib

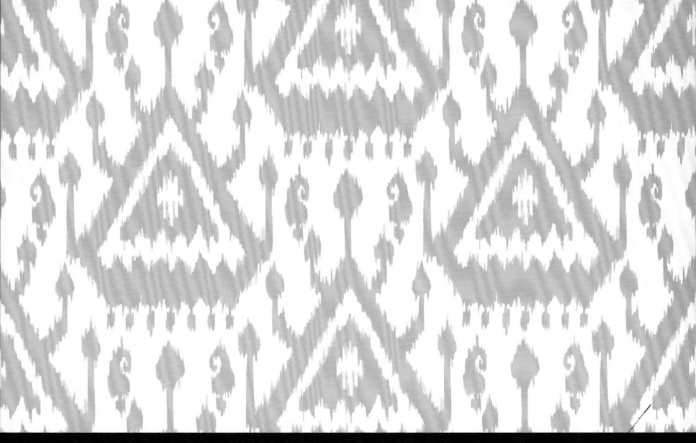

Vientiane Ikat in Palm from Schumacher

Pitaya in Rose
from Pierre Frey

153

Abstract

The undefined shapes of abstract patterns can resonate as much as an abstract painting: they give added presence without over-committing to a particular style or mood. Abstract pattern gives a space panache and yet leaves room for the imagination to play.

"Through the use of abstract pattern, one seeks to diverge from reality," says New York-based interior designer Patrick Mele. "The 'reality' of four plain walls, a ceiling, and a floor can be transformed into the paradise of a tropical garden, the skin of a leopard, the shoots of a bamboo forest. Abstracted designs, as in fine art, blur the lines even further and ask the inhabitant or visitor to question. Pattern, whether used in upholstery or affixed to a wall, has the power to trick the eye and to mask the truth."

The shapes within can be indescribable and don't fall into a predetermined format: a pattern may have a feeling of flowers, yet not quite be a floral. The shapes can be strong enough to feel geometric, yet not be dependable enough in their repeat to qualify as one. It's their indeterminate quality that gives abstracts their unique power. Abstracts can be used anywhere, in any kind of way, adding an invaluable layer of interest to your wall, window, or furniture.

"I love abstract patterns and like to combine them with figurative patterns for contrast and dynamism," says New York-based textile and interior designer Young Huh. "I am especially drawn toward patterns that come from, or are inspired by, Islamic decorative arts. The human mind loves mathematical patterns. I think we actually relate to them on a visceral and intuitive level because math and proportion are everywhere in nature." If you love pattern but feel unsure of which design direction to follow, the enigmatic qualities of abstract pattern can offer both fantasy and function.

Background: Yucatan in Fuschia from Pierre Frey

Inset: Queen of Spain in Black from Schumacher can turn a small bathroom into a design destination with its artful brushstrokes that never tire the eye. Interior design by Vaughn Miller Studio.

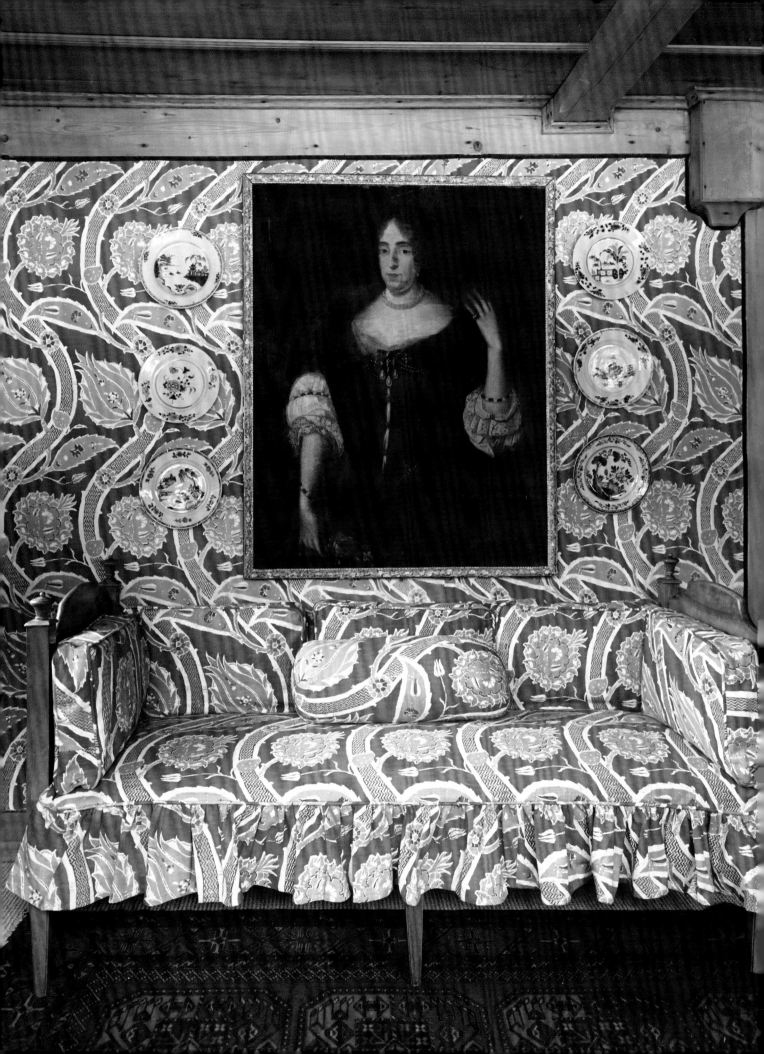

Bedrooms are the ideal place to use pattern
(here, Sherazade by Rubelli) both as a wall covering
and on the bed linens. It's a way to create a space
for sleeping that feels serene but not somnolent.
Interior design by Windsor Smith.

Opposite: Michelle Nussbaumer used her Sultana pattern
on both her wall and furniture to create a foundation
for layering that is at once seamless and whimsical.

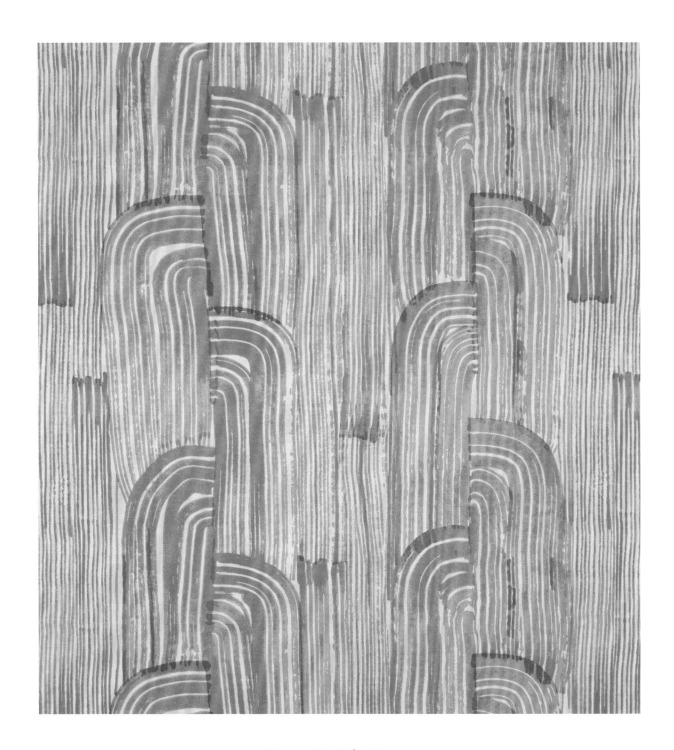

Crescent in Lake Cream
from Kelly Wearstler

Kelly Wearstler's Crescent lends not just pattern
to a bedroom but movement, thereby making the space
feel larger than it is. And it's a great companion to
modern furniture when you don't want to use something
too traditional. Interior design by Sheldon Harte.

Malachite in Green
from Jonathan Adler

Patterns always elevate their surrounding materials.
Here, Jonathan Adler's Malachite wallpaper in Grey enriches
velvet and gold tones. Interior design by Jonathan Adler.

In a Los Angeles home, patterns (here,
Minnie Maharani in Ruby by Peter Dunham
Textiles) bring a decidedly bohemian
feel just by nature of their casual charm.
Interior design by Peter Dunham.

Bukhara in Turquoise and Raspberry
from Peter Dunham Textiles

Abstract patterns can mix with stripes as long as they
are in the same color world. Here, Peter Dunham
used his Bukhara in Blue/Blue in his own bedroom.
Ironically, it makes the small space feel bigger and bolder
thanks to the dueling, yet compatible patterns.

Lotus in Fennel
from Galbraith & Paul

Pattern that isn't too specific in nature is just the trick
to mask tricky ceiling angles. Just add yummy color
(here, Lotus in Orange from Galbraith & Paul) to go from
funky to fabulous. Interior design by Colleen Bashaw.

Lotus in Black/Blue
from Farrow & Ball

"A powder room is the perfect place to take a design risk
with bold patterns," says designer Sue De Chiara. "This
Lotus print from Farrow & Ball was a longtime favorite of mine,
so I was thrilled to finally use it in our powder room. The
black trim and brass accents enhance the whole jewel box vibe."
Interior design by Sue De Chiara and Lauren Muse.

Shock Wave in Ruby
from Schumacher

Bargello in Bay and Cream from Peter Fasano   Agate in Lake Brown from Kelly Wearstler

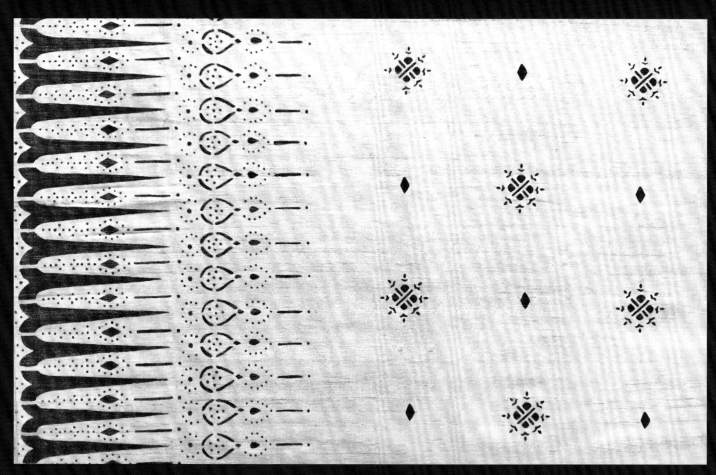

Kashmir in Ruby by Pintura Studio from Studio Four NYC

Pomegranate in Tomato from Galbraith & Paul

Castanet Embroidery in Red from Schumacher

Kayla in Rose Indien
by Manuel Canovas from Cowtan & Tout

175

Bruyère in Weld
from Fromental

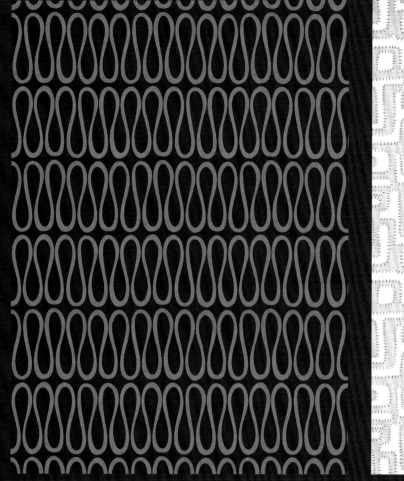

Bodoni in Espresso by Jonathan Adler for Kravet

Arizona in Charcoal Grey on Oyster
from Bennison Fabrics

Cupar in Walnut from Peter Fasano

Geometric

Whether it's triangles, squares, circles, or zigzags, the power of geometric patterns doesn't necessarily come from their shapes, but rather their repetition. Like the confident yet considerate dinner party guest, a geometric pattern brings immediate personality to its placement but never overwhelms due to its dependable DNA. "I've always loved bold geometrics because I've always loved bold floral and bold colors. At a certain point, one needs to balance boldness with boldness and geometric patterns achieve this splendidly," says San Francisco-based interior and textile designer Scot Meacham Woods.

Geometric patterns should never be confined to too small of an area: these kinds of patterns like to spread out and are ideal for covering an entire wall or floor and can ground a room as much as invigorate it, often breaking up careful symmetry of surrounding furniture in impactful ways. "The shape of something, and the way your eye and your spirit react to it, is as important to the soul of a room as the color on its walls, says Los Angeles-based interior and textile designer Kelly Wearstler. "Lines and geometric patterns represent the purity of form yet can be reinterpreted to exude a distinguishing spirit of originality and refinement. I love the beauty inherent in repetition and relaxed, geometric patterns. They bring rich dimension to every environment."

Background: Bamboo Wallpaper in Straw and Red from Cowtan & Tout

Inset: The height and drama of this stair hall in the country retreat she shares and designed with her husband, the architect Peter Pennoyer, inspired designer Katie Ridder to create Scraffito wallpaper, which mimics stone blocks and creates order while not taking itself too seriously.

Designer Kelly Behun uses Schumacher's Fez in Lapis to make the approach as much a destination as the bedroom itself. "I chose this paper for an overseas client's Manhattan pied-à-terre because it feels like life in New York, where people are always zigging or zagging somewhere and yet somehow miraculously not running headlong into each other. I find it exhilarating."

Opposite: Pattern can be practical, no matter how dramatic. "What looks to be wallpaper is actually a design painted freehand, in white and gray, over a matte black background," says designer Nick Olsen of this room. "The 'rustication' block pattern here complements other neoclassical elements in the space and helps disguise some irregular proportions we inherited from a previous renovation."

"Putting Pierre Frey's Haikou on the wall gave me the illusion of
sleeping in a tent, or inside a giant sweater," says designer Dirk Jan
Kinet. "It's embracingly beautiful and its colors make me sleep faster
and deeper." With Cole and Son's Apex Grand on the wardrobe doors.

Opposite: Give strong geometrics the breathing room to be gorgeous
by pairing them with a white ceiling. Here the pattern is Nante by
Brian Paquette for Studio Four NYC. Interior design by Kate Reynolds.

"Every room can use a wee bit of tartan!" is Scot Meacham
Wood's mantra and here he layers his Meacham Tartan
pattern as a foundation for other tartans to play against.

Opposite: "I practically use tartan as a neutral," says designer
Scot Meacham Wood. "It mixes amazingly well with bold
florals and modern geometrics." The sofa is in his Blackwatch
Tartan with a custom Buchanan Tartan Pillow.

Nebaha Embroidery in Citron
by Martyn Lawrence Bullard for Schumacher

As long as the colorways are complementary, geometric
patterns (Nebaha Embroidery from Martyn Lawrence Bullard
for Schumacher) can work with florals (Sinhala from
Martyn Lawrence Bullard for Schumacher) and even ikats
(Dayra by Martyn Lawrence Bullard for Schumacher).

Golden Sunburst in Starlight Blue, Jim
Thompson Fabrics, Tony Duquette Collection

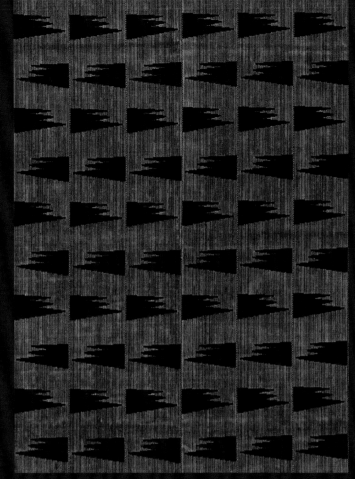

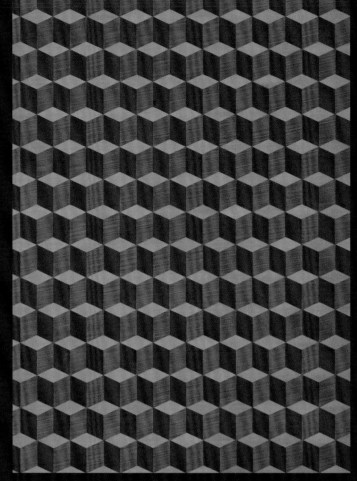

Tutsi in Green by David Kaihoi for Schumacher

Legno in Maple by Angolo & Legno for Schumacher

Cosmos II in Navy and Red by Studio Bon for Schumacher

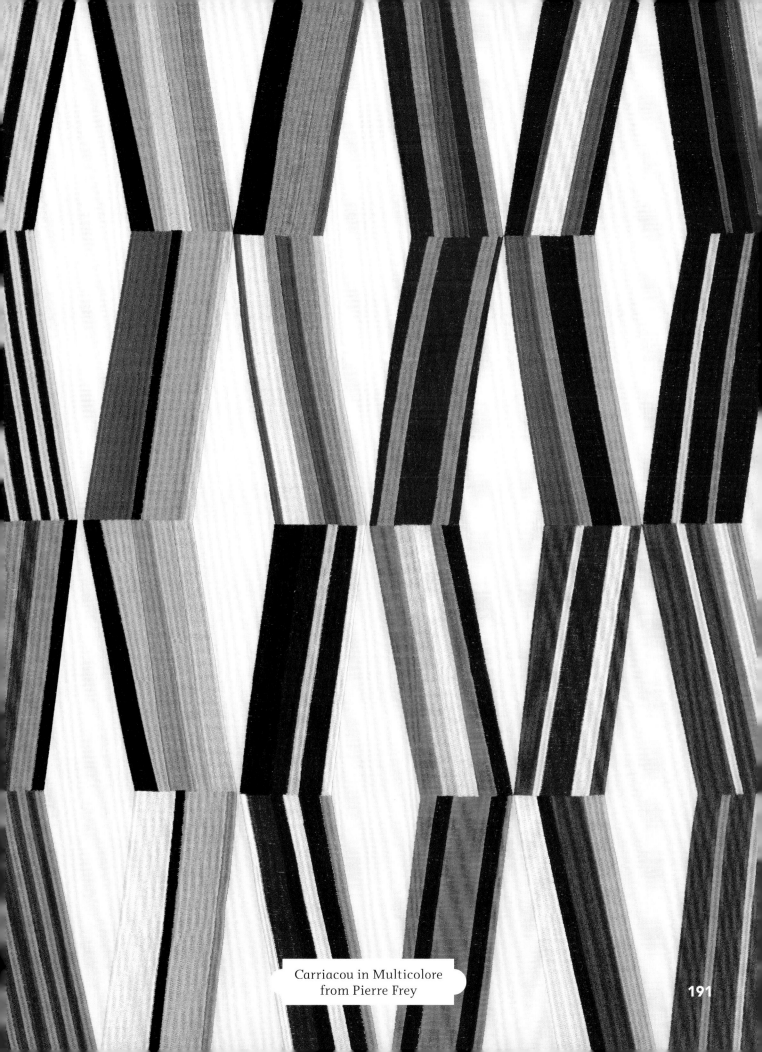

Carriacou in Multicolore
from Pierre Frey

192

Amazed in Hibiscus
from Scalamandre

Cayman in Green
by Serena & Lily

194

Samovar in Peacock by Martyn Lawrence Bullard
for Schumacher

Pompeian from Cole and Son

Bleecker in Peacock from Schumacher

Stripes

Ever since America's first professional interior designer, Elsie de Wolfe, donned stripes on the dance pavilion at her weekend retreat chez Villa Trianon at Versailles in the late 1920s, stripes have proved themselves to be the perfect party guest: dependable yet bold, distinct, yet able to mix with any pattern personality, no matter the occasion. Whether it's in the classic crisp pairing of blue-and-white stripes, the modern punch of wide black-and-white stripes, or the playful mix of tricolored stripes, the constant is the uplifting mood they give, whether down a stairway runner, on a child's headboard, covering a living room wall or a throw pillow.

"I layered oodles of stripes in my own bedroom because they make me so happy," says interior designer Sam Allen. "Stripes are cheerful and bright and make a room feel crisp and clean." They can also make it feel bigger. "Stripes help elongate, heighten, and lengthen spaces," says New York interior and textile designer Sheila Bridges. "They create a type of visual organization and an illusion that walls are taller than they are."

Stripes don't always have to be bands of solid color: they can manifest their steadfast format in more mysterious ways, like the parallel rows of Schumacher's Zebra Palm fronds, or the flower-filled stripes of Lee Jofa's Shalimar Stripe, or the exotic elegance of Peter Dunham's Isfahan Stripe. Just when you think you've seen them all, another stripe is sure to come along, charming its way, deservedly, into the mix.

Background: Versa in Tutti Frutti from Madeline Weinrib

Inset: Stripes can give floral patterns more gravitas, while still letting them shine. Here, the black and whites act almost as a neutral and become the ideal floral foil. Interior design by Meredith German and Barrie Benson. (Originally appeared in *Good Bones, Great Pieces* by Suzanne and Lauren McGrath.)

The Classic Stripe Wallpaper from Sheila Bridges has a refreshing formality to its unique colorway, reminding us that stripes needn't be relegated to just navy and white. Interior design by Sheila Bridges.

Damascus Stripe in Ruby Emerald
from Soane Britain

Damascus Stripe in Ruby Emerald from Soane
Britain proves that a thin stripe can give off a vibe
as wonderfully casual and cozy as a lit fireplace.
Interior design by Lulu Lytle.

Stripes are ideal for leading the way up, down, and across hallways via runners and can even join two solids with panache. Custom rugs from Patterson Flynn Martin. Interior design by Vaughn Miller Studio.

Opposite: Designer Alex Papachristidis sheathed Lee Jofa's Luxembourg stripe in Teal and Plum to create a tented effect in his Manhattan entryway: an ingenious way to chicly give an illusion of space and delight the eye.

Mrs. Howard Room by Room PHOEBE HOWARD

BEAUTY AT HOME AERIN LAUDER

INSPIRATIONS *from* FRANCE & ITALY PHILLIPS

Acanthus Stripe in Turmeric by Celerie Kemble
for Schumacher

A stripe doesn't necessarily mean two straight lines:
it's the journey and shape that give extra distinction
to any wall. Here it's Acanthus Stripe in Shadow
by Celerie Kemble from Schumacher. Interior design
by R. Cartwright Design.

Above: Designer Cathy Kincaid uses stripes on antique chairs
to keep pace with the patterns on the walls and floors.

Opposite: Designer Frank de Biasi turned inexpensive
mattress ticking into the blue-and-white stripe that he
craved and paired it with vintage wallpaper with
purple trim for a customized wall that feels as deeply
personal as his collections.

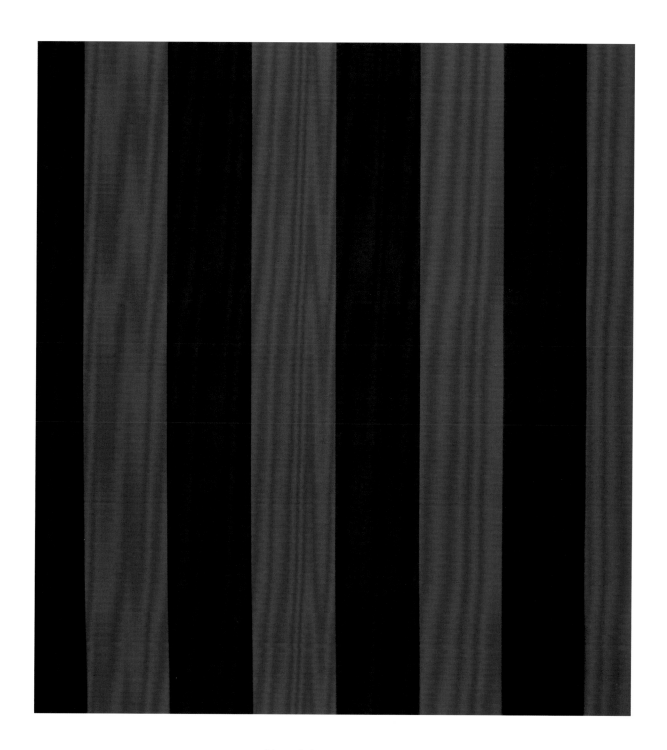

Stubbs Club Stripe in Riviera
by Ralph Lauren Home

Bold stripes can be layered just as effectively as florals and
shouldn't be limited to only entry halls and sunporches.
Here the pattern on the walls and headboard is
Lighthouse Stripe by Ralph Lauren Home in White/Navy.
Interior design by Sam Allen.

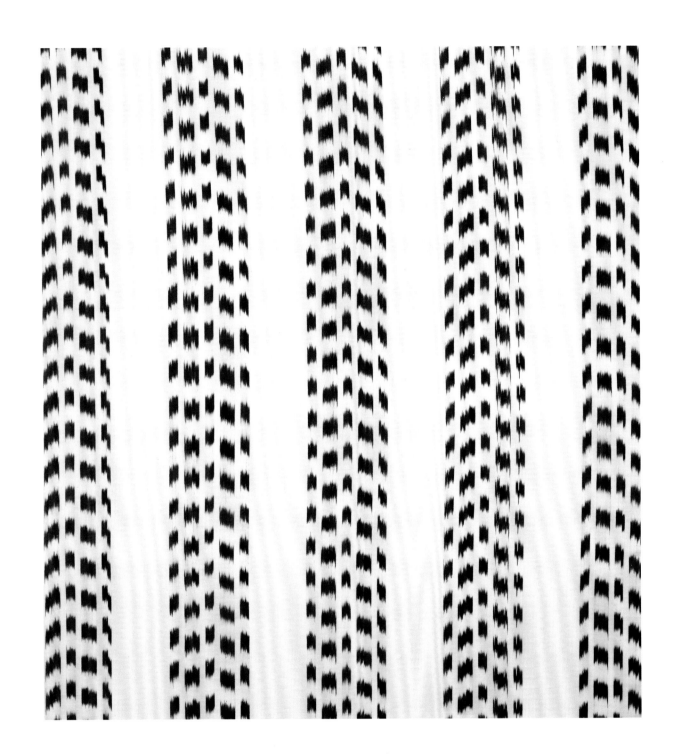

Izmir Stripe in Indigo
from Schumacher

Izmir Stripe in Indigo from Schumacher is the ideal stripe
to weave into a room full of exotic textures and patterns.
It completely holds its own while blending into the
marvelous mix. Interior design by William R. McLure IV.

SIMPLICITY NANCY BRAITHWAITE

212

Tikal in Multicolore
from Pierre Frey

213

Pippin Stripe in Purple from Clarence House

Wide Stripe in Bottle Green on Beige
from Bennison Fabrics

Wicker Stripe in Licorice by Celerie Kemble for Schumacher

Branca Stripe in Rouge by Alessandra Branca
for Schumacher

215

Antique Ticking Stripe in Denim
from Schumacher

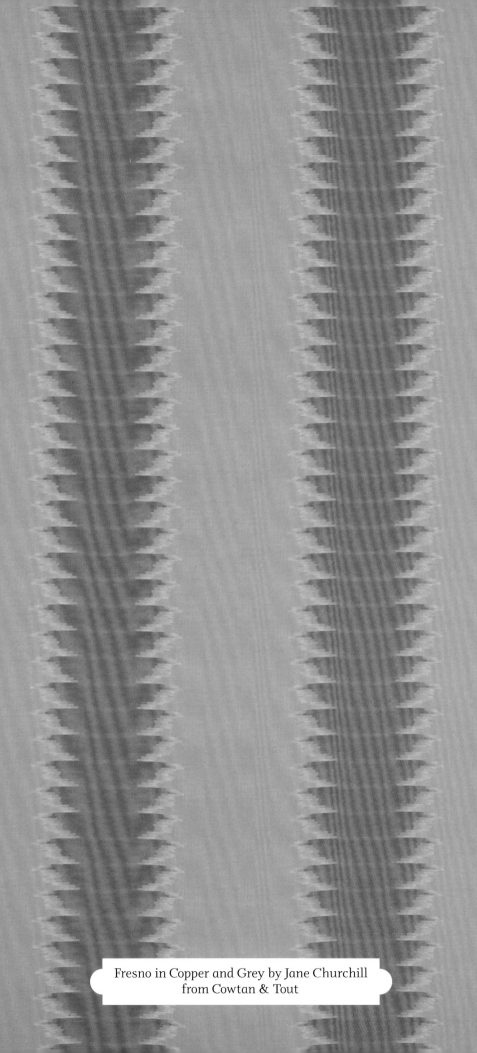

Fresno in Copper and Grey by Jane Churchill
from Cowtan & Tout

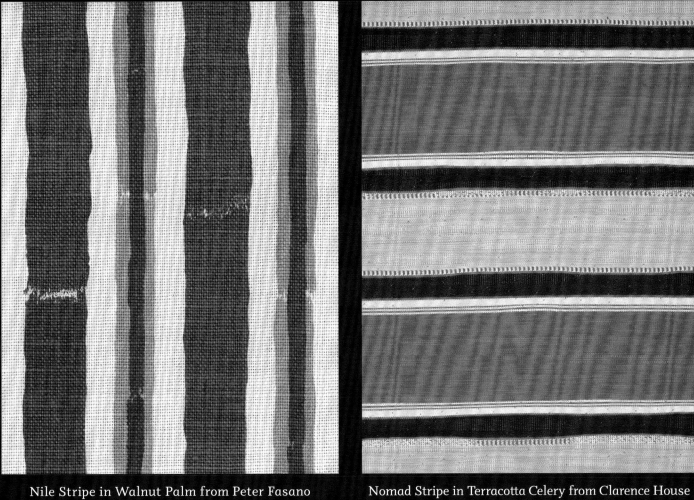

Nile Stripe in Walnut Palm from Peter Fasano

Nomad Stripe in Terracotta Celery from Clarence House

La Païva in Multicolore from the Braquenie Collection by Pierre Frey

Iconic

CHAPTER
12

"To be iconic, you need to stand the test of time," says Schumacher's creative director Dara Caponigro. "The reason some things stick around while others don't has to do with how thoughtfully they were designed. Whether something is classic or contemporary, if it isn't imbued with knowledge of what came before and a deep understanding of what it is meant to be or do, it won't make it. Gimmicky never wins."

Common characteristics of iconic patterns are conflicting yet compatible: a design that is both timeless but always feels of the moment; a design that has an ego yet plays very well with others. "I've always loved decorating with iconic fabrics," says New York–based interior designer Nick Olsen. "A Madeleine Castaing *rayure*, Paule Marrot floral, or Alan Campbell block print, to name a few, for the sense of timelessness and connoisseurship they give any room. But it's all in the execution. I may not replicate Mario Buatta's famed "Toile de Nantes" canopy bed, and opt instead for a Marrot-print refrigerator. Yes, I wallpapered my first fridge! I also find that iconic prints, especially hand block floral chintzes, have such interesting color combinations that a single Jean Monro throw can set the color palette for an entire room." Even though some of these iconic patterns have been around for more than fifty years, and we've seen them

repeatedly in movies or in magazines, show houses or our friend's powder rooms, they somehow never overstay their welcome.

Whether possessing the overt sparkle of Scalamandre's Zebras, or Fireworks from Hinson by Donghia, or the quiet panache of Cole and Son's Woods or Brunschwig & Fils's Les Touches, these style icons have staying power because they exude that *je ne sais quoi* and beauty that we so often associate with movie stars. Just as it's hard to ever tire of looking at Cary Grant or Cate Blanchett whenever they come on-screen, the same could be said of walking into a room and being greeted by Lee Jofa's Hollyhock or Sandberg's Raphaël.

"Iconic patterns create a connection to the great style makers and decorators that came before us and bring these distinctive designs into the future for the next generation to enjoy," says New York–based interior designer Ashley Whittaker. "Whether it's the eighteenth-century chinoiserie paper in Pauline de Rothschild's Paris bedroom or the Brunschwig & Fils La Portugaise famously used by Albert Hadley in Brooke Astor's library, these patterns stand the test of time. Iconic patterns bring an instant sense of history, familiarity, and comfort belonging to any room. They feel as relevant today as they did when they were originally designed."

Background: Tibet Small Scale in Navy from Clarence House

Inset: Carolyne Roehm uses Le Grand Genois-Panneau from the Braquenie Collection by Pierre Frey in abundance in her guest room. The Tree of Life was a popular eighteenth-century French design and, as this version is available in various coordinates, it can be used in the classic French way of repeating the pattern throughout the room.

220

Chiang Mai Dragon in Aquamarine
from Schumacher

"This art deco-based print is vibrant, optimistic, and
absolutely timeless," says designer Shelly Rosenberg of
Schumacher's Chiang Mai Dragon (which she used here
in Aquamarine.) "A little packs a real punch or you can
go full bore and do an entire room for maximum impact!"

Fireworks in Black on Off White
from Hinson by Donghia

Christopher Spitzmiller used the Fireworks pattern (created by legendary designer
Albert Hadley together with Harry Hinson) in his guest room in a way that feels
both fresh and reverential. "I love everything Albert Hadley, his mark is all over
my house. Every bedroom has one of his wallpapers. Fireworks in red dots that
form a pattern of fireworks exploding is the perfect contrast to the painted blue floor.
I'm all about the contrast. Certain guests won't sleep in any other bedroom!"
Interior design by Harry Heissmann and Christopher Spitzmiller.

"I've always adored Abre de Matisse from China Seas for Quadrille and its spirited homage to nature," says designer Patrick Mele, who uses the Brown on Tint here in a guest bedroom. "Billy Baldwin created a singular fabric, adapted from Henri Matisse's masterful yet naive brushtrokes, that breathes life into any room."

The Vase in Navy and Blue
from Clarence House

Designer Philip Gorrivan employed the Vase in Taupe
and White from Clarence House to give extra dimension to
a hallway's glamorous vignette of accessories.

Citrus Garden in Primary
from Schumacher

Schumacher's Citrus Garden in Primary always makes
everything look alive and fresh, no matter its age or origin.

Hollyhock in White/Brown
from Lee Jofa

When paired with velvets and lush leopards,
Lee Jofa's Hollyhock transcends its chintz cult status to
become a team player. Interior design by Young Huh.

Flowering Quince in Black
from Clarence House

No matter what wall it graces and where, Flowering
Quince from Clarence House can look edgy,
whimsical, and classic all at once, the mark of a true icon.
Interior design by Lisa Borgnes Giramonti.

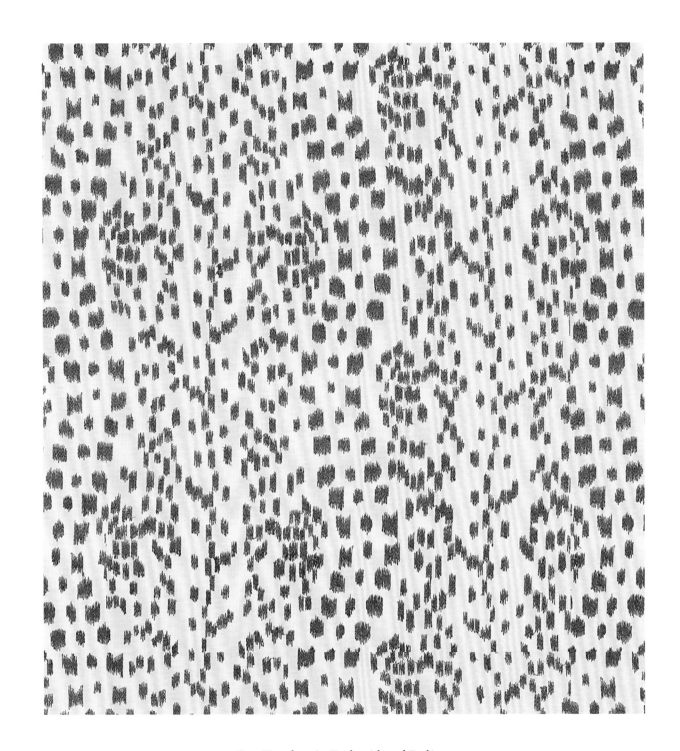

Les Touches in Embroidered Indigo
from Brunschwig & Fils

Les Touches from Brunschwig & Fils is always recognizable
yet seems to give a distinctive touch to whatever
room it's in, delighting the beholders no matter their age.
Interior design by Amy Corrigan.

Zebrine in Blue and White
from Rose Cumming

"Is there anything more timeless than an animal print?" asks
designer Ashley Whittaker. "Even in this out-of-the-ordinary navy
blue hue I've used here, this pattern is grounded in history.
Designed by legendary decorator Rose Cumming in the 1930s for the
ultrachic nightclub El Morocco, this iconic paper is a modern
workhorse that serves as one of my all-time favorite backdrops."

Raphaël in Blue
from Sandberg Wallpaper

"Raphaël from Sandberg is iconic in its familiarity yet always feels so fresh and new," says designer Grant K. Gibson. "I love how it's unexpected in this kitchen area with the blue and greens, yet traditional and classic at the same time. The branches give it a dreamlike quality."

Fig Leaf in Original on White from Peter Dunham Textiles

Manor Rose in Nightfall by Dorothy Draper for Schumacher

Dorothy Draper protégé (and president of Dorothy Draper & Company) Carleton Varney reminded everyone of the enduring fabulousness of Draper's own Brazilliance pattern when he revamped the famed Greenbrier Hotel in West Virginia.

244

Delphinium
by Rose Cumming

St. Laurent on custom Blue India Tea Paper
from de Gournay

Woods from Cole and Son

Décor Chinois in Rose from Zuber & Cie

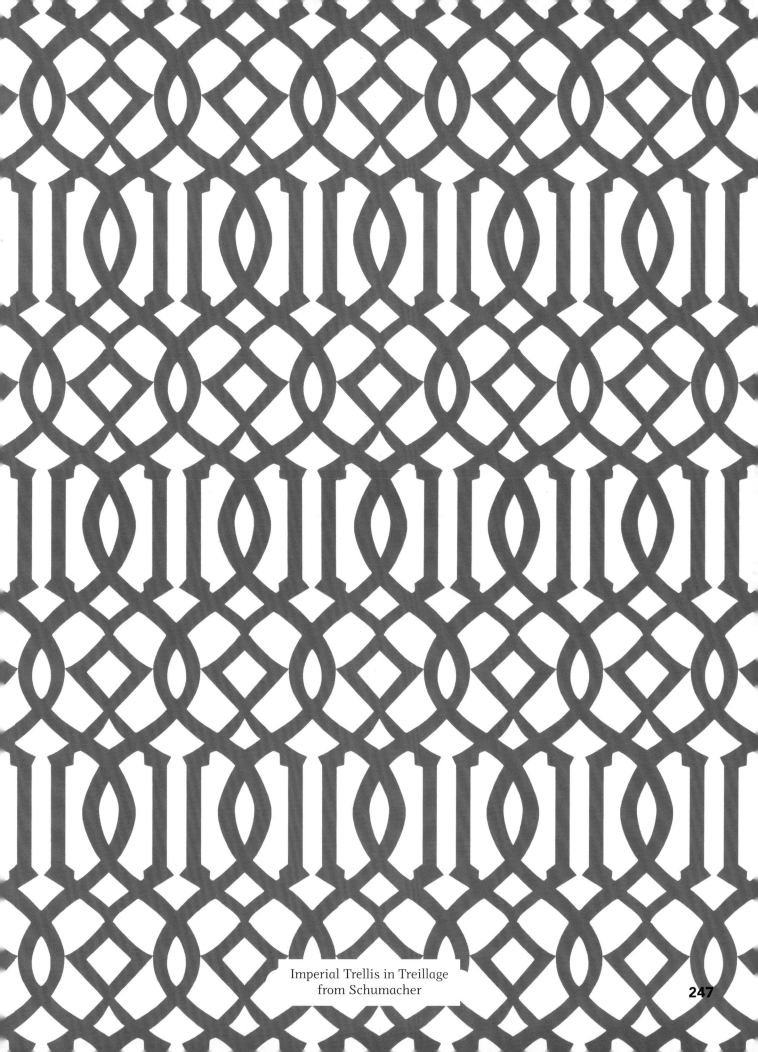

Imperial Trellis in Treillage
from Schumacher

Hicks' Hexagon in Gilver, White, and Black from Cole and Son

Exposition Universelle in Garance from the Braquenie Collection by Pierre Frey

Iconic Leopard in Fuchsia Natural
from Schumacher

250

Designer Credits

Deconstructed Stripe in Red
by Miles Redd for Schumacher

Photographer Credits

Ambria in Corail by Manuel Canovas from Cowtan & Tout

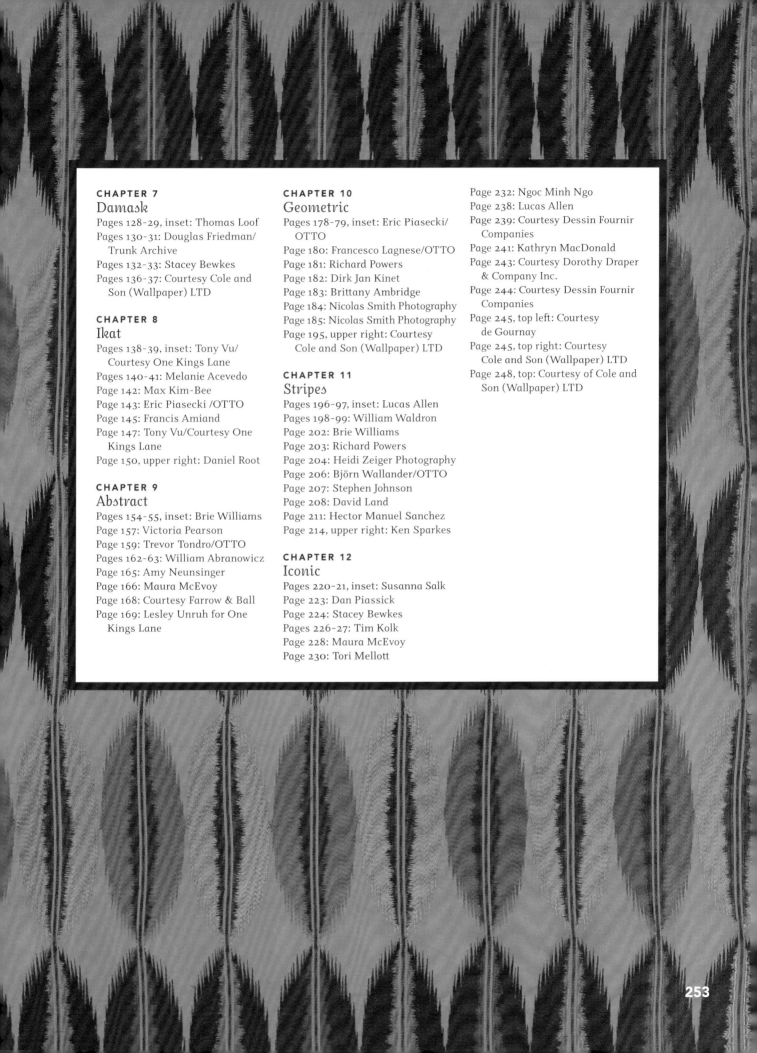

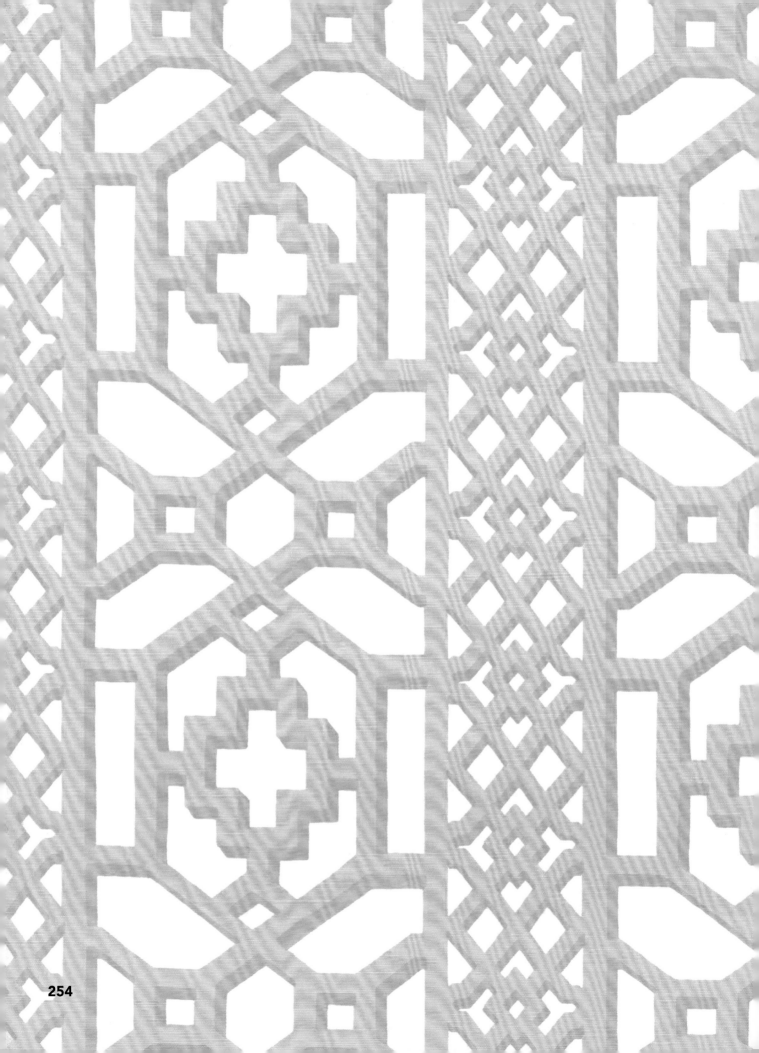

254

acknowledgments

As always, my amazing Rizzoli editor, Ellen Nidy, got my idea to showcase pattern up close and personal from the get-go. Our almost telepathic way of communicating makes the hard work feel like the privilege that it is.

Our fearless art director Kayleigh Jankowski nailed our unusual layout before we knew what had happened, translating it from my jumbled words to gorgeousness on paper. Her vision was perhaps the driving force and shape of this book. Plus I knew from the moment I saw her avocado tattoo that she was going to be special!

A special thanks to my partner in design crime Stacey Bewkes for so generously lending some of her magnificent photos.

Thanks to Dara Caponigro for supporting my idea for this book from the beginning, with both her enthusiasm and smarts, as well as so many Schumacher images.

And to all the textile houses showcased within: it was an honor to celebrate your archives, both past and present, and to give you the spotlight and space you so deserve!

To all the amazing interior designers whose work we feature here and whose words equally inspire, thank you. You bring so much craft, creativity, and CHIC into all our lives.

Zanzibar Trellis Matte in Canary
from Schumacher

First published in the United
States of America in 2018 by
Rizzoli International Publications, Inc.
300 Park Avenue South
New York, NY 10010
www.rizzoliusa.com

Design: Kayleigh Jankowski | Rizzoli editor: Ellen Nidy

2018 2019 2020 2021 2022 / 10 9 8 7 6 5 4 3 2 1
ISBN-13: 978-0-8478-6289-4
Library of Congress Control Number: 2018941590

Printed and bound in China
Distributed to the U.S. trade by Random House

Page 1: Zebras in Red by Scalamandre
Pages 2-3: Miles Redd cocoons a family room in exotic pattern
to make it feel at once worldly and homey via Schumacher's
Samarkand Ikat II in Porcelain on the furniture and
Iksel's Iznik Charpi on its walls. "Iznik Charpi is indicative
of the sophistication of the Ottoman Empire," says Redd.
"I love how something from the fifteenth century can
mix so well with contemporary art and look fresh
and modern today. It goes to show you,
great design will always mix well
with other great design."

Hand-painted Earlham design on Emerald
Green dyed silk from de Gournay